PRELUDE

You're trying your best to move on, but you just can't get over something that happened to you in your past. It's something that changed you and your life forever. It's something that keeps bothering you and making you miserable. You'd love to get over it, but how can you get over something that caused you so much pain? Just thinking about your past brings tears to your eyes and pain to your heart. How can you fix a heart that has been broken beyond repair? How can you move on when what happened to you caused you so much pain? How can you ever forget that day when they hurt you, broke your heart or took advantage of you? Well, you'll never forget it, but you can move on. This guide will help those who have been hurt in their past to move on.

This guide is for those who have been hurt by someone in their past. While it can be used for breakups, it's directed towards those that have suffered from abuse, abusive relationships, bad relationships where they were used or taken advantage of, domestic violence, neglect, childhood trauma, rape, violence, sexual molestation or other similar things. If you need help letting go of someone you love; '25 Steps to Letting Go of Someone You Love' is better suited for you.

Table of Contents

This book wasn't written by someone with a perfect past, it was written by someone with a disturbing, troubled past. I'm telling you this because I believe that the best person to help you get through something is someone that has already been through hell and made it through it. Before I turned 12 I had experienced almost everything a woman fears and I'd been hurt more times than I could count. Rape, molestation, neglect, physical abuse and verbal abuse, you name it. Because of the neglect I was taken from my biological mother and placed into the foster care system, and from there I went from foster home to foster home. However, it didn't take long for me to realize that foster homes were just as bad as my mother's home. In fact, the bulk of the things that happened to me occurred while I was in the foster care system. Well, fast-forward to the present and I'm sitting here writing to you, hoping that I can help you to move on, just as I have. How did I go from the foster care system to achieving my hopes and dreams? Why didn't I give up after all that I've been through? This guide will tell you what worked for me.

Over the years, I've given advice to hundreds of people and the first thing I say to them is that they've already taken the first step. Realizing or admitting that you have a problem is the first step and seeking help is the second step. The fact that you are reading this book, and trying to figure out how to move on means that you are mentally ready to move on with your life and that you've taken the first two steps. You're ready to let go. You are ready to release all of your pain. You're sick of crying over and over again about the same thing. You want your life back. You want to be happy but you just can't seem to forget what they did to you. They hurt you and robbed you of so much. They stole something from you and you feel like you'll never get it back. What did they do to you? What happened? What did they do to you? What happened to you? They took advantage of your trust or your weaknesses and you're wondering why it happened to you. You wish you could forget about it, but it's too painful to forget. You have so much pain in your heart. Life has been so unfair to you and you're sick of people hurting you, using you or abusing you. Why do people do these things to you? Why? What have you done to deserve all of this pain! You wish people would stop hurting you. You just want to be happy.

Breathe in and breathe out, breathe in and breathe out and realize that, that part of your life is over and that today is the beginning of a new chapter in your life. The chapter where you finally move on and realize that life isn't so bad. Are you ready to move on? Mark this day on your calendar.

You deserve peace, love, happiness and all that your heart desires. Don't let anyone control your life and take away those things.

FLASHBACKS

Do you understand how it feels to have flashbacks that paralyze you and make you relive parts of your life that you'd love to forget? Do you know how it feels to want to die, and just end it all? Do you know how it feels to feel like you're unlucky, and like everything bad keeps happening to you? Do you know how it feels to hate yourself, and your life? Do you know how it feels to feel out of control or like you're a prisoner of the past? The past keeps replaying itself over and over again. It's like you're constantly watching this horror movie or never ending bad movie starring you as the main character. You're constantly watching this movie, and you wish you could stop it from replaying the same part over and over again. Yet it keeps playing the parts of your life where you were hurt, and you were in pain. Every time you try to move on, the flashbacks bring you back to square one again. Something in the present always triggers an old memory, and you drift off into your past again. One minute you're in the present, and the next you're stuck in the past watching yourself be hurt all over again. The pain you feel when you have these flashbacks feels as if you're being hurt again. It feels like someone is stabbing you in your heart, and you enter into somewhat of a trance.

I once had a flashback that sent me spiraling back into my past and caused me to fall to my knees crying, uncontrollably. After traumatic events, flashbacks are normal and expected but once you move on they'll be extremely rare and less painful. I can now, tell my story without breaking down into tears or reliving the moment. That will come to you in time.

I can see the pain in your eyes. Physically you're sitting right in front of me, but mentally you've drifted off into your miserable past.

If the above describes you this book was written for you.

When was your last flashback?

What triggers your flashbacks?

How do you usually feel after a flashback?

After a flashback, how long does it take you to regain control of yourself?

Do your flashbacks make you cry?

After you have a flashback, write down how you feel and then switch to an uplifting activity. Writing down how you feel helps you to deal with a flashback and the emotions it brings to the surface.

The pain

After you're hurt by someone you're in so much pain. Heartbreaking, life changing, brings you to your knees in tears type of pain. Emotionally you experience every emotion known to men, and you might even break down. Physically you feel weak, and you feel as if you're drained or empty. Mentally you keep replaying what happened to you over and over again trying to make sense of it all. You want to know why they hurt you. You want to know why it happened to you. You feel as if your life might be over, and that you'll never recover from the pain. You feel as if things will never be the same, and that you'll never be happy again. Also, you wish you could go back to that day, and do something differently. Something that would have stopped them from hurting you. You might even blame yourself for what they did to you. You think that something you did or said caused them to hurt you. So many things are floating through your head, the past keeps haunting you, and your emotions go up and down. One minute you're happy, and the next you're sad because of a flashback. How can you move on from a life changing event? I'm hoping that I can help you on your journey to moving on. Grab a journal, and let's get started.

THE PART OF YOUR LIFE THAT YOU CAN'T GET OVER

In order to move on, you need to start from the beginning. Most likely, you've repressed what happened to you and you haven't dealt with it fully and completely.

Grab a pen and paper, and answer the following questions:

1. What happened to you in your past that is so hard for you to get over?

2. What brings tears to your eyes every time you think about it?

3. Who in your past are you mad at?

4. Who do you want to get revenge on?

5. Who changed you into someone that you're not?

6. Who hurt you?

7. Who made your life so miserable?

8. How did it make you feel?

9. Do you want revenge? If so, what kind?

10. Do you blame yourself? If so, why?

Below, write down everything that comes to your mind. Write your complete story, and don't leave anything out. Let your mind guide the pen or pencil that you're holding. This is an important step. You must release all of your thoughts surrounding your experience. The good, the bad and those secrets that only you know. Write it all down.

Every time you think about your past you feel pain. However, you should also be proud of yourself because even though that was one of the hardest things you have ever had to go through you made it through it. That's right you made it through it. How did you make it through the hardest parts of your life? How did you get out of bed every morning since then? How in the world did you survive your past? It's because you're strong. That's the only logical explanation.

Now, let's go to step one in your journey to letting go

STEP ONE

Is to admit that it happened to you. Don't pretend like it didn't happen to you. Don't make excuses for what happened to you, and don't be ashamed of what happened to you. The main reason some people never move on is because they've never faced their past. Since the day they were hurt they've tried to block out their past or pretend like it never happened. They think they have to be strong, and that feeling weak or vulnerable because of their past makes them a weak person. Realize that feeling week or vulnerable after you're hurt is normal, and it makes you a normal person, not a weak person. However, blocking out your past doesn't help you to move on, it's just a temporary fix. It's temporary because as soon as a memory pops into your head it reminds you that you haven't moved on and that you're just pretending to be okay. Starting today, you have to face your past and face the realities of what happened to you. What happened to you is that someone hurt you, and since the day they hurt you, you've tried to block out what happened to you instead of facing it. They hurt you, your past makes you miserable, and you're sad because of your past. To face your past, you have to face yourself, and how you really feel about the past. What happened to you in the past is a miserable part of your past, but it's still a part of your past. Everything that happens to you whether it's good or bad is a part of your life story. If your life were a book and people were reading it they would want to know every part of your life story, and they would want to know what you did after you were hurt. Whenever you watch a sad movie about someone's life, you hope they have a happy ending. You hope they defeat their enemies, overcome their past, and find a way to be happy. Well, you've had something bad happen to you, and you have to fight so that you can have a happy ending. Make your life story great. Make it a story where you defeated your enemies, overcame your past, and you had a happy ending. In order to do this, you have to stop running from your past, and stop trying to block out those bad memories. Once you stop running from your past it won't control you anymore because you're no longer afraid or ashamed of it.

Go look at yourself in your mirror. Look at yourself in your eyes, and face yourself. Once you do this you are facing your past instead of running from it. In order for this to work you have to look into your mirror and look into your eyes; if you don't you're not facing yourself. When you look into your eyes you can't hide how you feel. Your eyes will reveal everything; your eyes never lie. A fake smile can never hide the sad look in your eyes.

Before you go to step 2 you must complete the following assignment.

Assignment 1: Face your past:

Be 100% honest with yourself and don't hold anything back. Keep going until you're done with all 6 steps. Don't let tears, sadness or anger stop you from finishing the 6 steps below.

1. Look at yourself in the mirror
2. Admit that it happened to you
3. Tell yourself what happened to you
4. Tell yourself how it made you feel
5. Admit that it's still bothering you
6. Tell yourself what you think about the person who hurt you
7. If you don't have a mirror right now, come back to this step. It's important!

"You can pretend like you're fine and everything is okay, but until you deal with what's bothering you the pain won't go away"

Suicidal thoughts

A person that is in too much pain. Pain that they can't deal with or handle might consider suicide. Suicide is the only thing they can think of that will get rid of all their pain and problems. They think suicide is the only way to stop their pain and suffering. To them what happened to them ended their life, and there's no point in living anymore. Some people aren't as strong as others, and they just can't handle the evilness that comes into their life. I want you to know that there is another way to deal with the pain besides committing suicide. The other way is to keep fighting. I know you think you can't fight anymore or that it's too hard to fight, but I want you to try anyway. If you keep fighting, you'll realize that there is a light at the end of the tunnel. Also, you'll realize that you can defeat your past and that you can defeat your enemies. If you fight you'll be happy again, and one day you'll be happy you never gave up. You might feel as if no-one cares about you, and that no-one will miss you, but that isn't true. Your family and friends will miss you, and committing suicide will cause them to feel pain as well. For those who don't have family or friends or anyone to talk to. Realize that you could have those things in your future. If you keep fighting and go out into the world you can meet new people. If you join a support group, you can meet people who have been through the same things you have. There are online forums filled with people that are experiencing the same pain that you feel. Join a group or forum and you'll be on your way to making new friends. If you fight great things will happen to you in your future. At one point I thought about ending my own life, but if I had done it I wouldn't have helped thousands of people. I wouldn't have accomplished a lot of my goals, and I would have missed out on so many good things in life. I'm living proof that happiness can come after misery. If I had committed suicide you wouldn't be reading this book right now because I would have died years ago. I know you think it's the end of the world for you, but I'm here to tell you that it isn't. Do me a favor, and just give life another chance. Promise me that you'll fight, and fight, and fight, and that you'll never give up. Don't throw away your life, use your life to make a difference in the world.

Have you ever had suicidal thoughts? If so, explain why and what happened.

They got away with it

Do you feel as if they got away with hurting you?

One of the worst feelings ever is knowing that the person who hurt you got away with it. It bothers you that they could get away with something that caused you so much misery. You replay the past in your head wishing that you could do something to them. Wishing that you could stop them from hurting you, defend yourself from them, or get revenge on them. You hate feeling helpless against them, and flashbacks always make you feel like a helpless victim. Every time you have a flashback you have to watch yourself be hurt, and you can't do anything to change what is taking place. Realize that the main reason you keep replaying your past is because you wish you could change it. If you could only defend yourself or stop them from hurting you it wouldn't have happened. Not being able to pay them back, stop them or punish them for what happened to you is keeping you stuck in the past. Realize that even though you couldn't stop them from hurting you in the past that you can stop them from messing up your future. Realize that moving on is the best way to get revenge on them.

When you move on:

- You're saying that you're taking your life back.
- That you're not giving up.
- That you're not going to let what they did destroy you.
- That you want to do whatever it takes for you to be happy again.
- That you're going to fix your broken spirit.

When you give up on life because of what they did to you:

- You're saying that your life belongs to them.

- That you've given up on happiness.
- That you're going to allow them to mess up your future.
- That you're going to stay broken forever.

If you're reading this eBook a part of you once to move on, and a part of you wants to see what else life has to offer you. Once you move on your life will belong to you again, and they will no longer control your life anymore. Realize that karma will punish them, and make them pay for what they did to you. I've watched Karma punish someone more than I ever thought they'd be punished and one of the people that hurt me is no longer living. Trust me, they'll get what's coming to them. You might not be able to see them being punished, but believe me, they will be punished. But for now, you need to move on and focus on getting your life back together. What happens to you NOW should be more important than what didn't happen to them before.

They're not worth your time

Realize that they don't deserve another second of your time. How many months or years have you given a person that doesn't deserve your attention? Have you given them 5, 10, 15 or 20 years of your life? If they really hurt you and messed up your life they've already wasted enough of your time. Right now they're in the past where they belong, and you need to leave them there. Leave them in the past, and stop dragging them around with you everywhere you go. They are holding you back and wasting time that you'll never get back. They don't deserve your time or anything else that you have. They're not worth giving up on everything for. They're not worth throwing your whole life away for. Don't let a person like that continue to mess up the only life that you'll ever have. This is your life, not theirs, but you're letting them waste your time. How many more months or years of your life are you going to give them? I think you should give yourself those months or years instead. Give yourself a chance to enjoy the rest of your life. Are you going to give a person like that the rest of your life? Are you going to give them another 5, 10 or 15 years of your life? If so, that's time that you'll never get back. It's time for you to start spending your time on yourself, and things that will make you happy. Don't give them another second of your time because you and I both know they don't deserve it. In fact, they never deserved a second of your time, and they might have stolen the time they did get.

Is the person that hurt you worth your time?

How many more years of your life are you going to give them?

You have to clean up the mess.

Some people will come into your life, and make a complete mess of things, but it's your job to clean it up. Before they came into your life you were in control of your life, and everything was going smoothly. Once they came into your life they messed things up, and you couldn't stop them from messing it up. You were helpless in that situation, and you felt like you were no longer in control of your life anymore. You watched them carelessly mess up your life, and at the moment you realized that others had the power to mess up something that was supposed to be yours. Your life was supposed to belong to you, and yet they were controlling it and messing it up. Not only were they controlling it, but you couldn't stop them from controlling it. You had to watch your life unfold as if you were an observer instead of a participant. After you watched them mess up your life you watched them walk away, and leave the mess behind. How dare they come into your life, mess things up, and then walk away like your feelings didn't matter? How dare they do something to you so hurtful, and then leave you to deal with it? How could someone be so heartless, evil or cruel to you when you didn't do anything to them? After they messed up your life you didn't clean it up, you just left it messy and broken. In fact, it's still messy and instead of cleaning It up, you just walk around the mess or avoid it. You pretend like the mess isn't there. The mess seems like too much to clean up, and the brokenness seems too hard to fix. Plus, it isn't fair that you have to clean up the mess that they made, and they shouldn't have messed it up in the first place. Also, your life changed that day because you no longer felt in control of it, and until you get back in control of it, you'll still feel like an observer instead of a participant. If you don't move on you'll continue to watch your life unfold or unravel on its own instead of participating in it. Also, when they left the mess they took your life with them, and they still have your life in the palm of their hands. They're dangling your life in front of your face, but you don't think you're strong enough to take it from them. So, you just leave things the way they are.

Who has to clean up the mess that they caused?

It isn't fair but you have to do it, it's the only way to get your life back.

Will you clean up the mess?

Close your eyes and picture them dangling your life back and forth in front of your face like it's a pendulum. Picture it dangling back and forth, and back and forth.

1. If you're too afraid to snatch it out of their hands you're still letting them control you, and you feel powerless.
2. If you take too long to snatch it you're still afraid of them, but you should realize that they can no longer hurt you and that you can stand up to them now. So, don't be afraid.
3. If you feel helpless or paralyzed, and like you can't do anything to stop them you're still being their victim. Realize that you're not their victim anymore and that you can stand up to them.
4. If you're just sitting there watching them dangle it back and forth and you're not even thinking about grabbing it you've gotten used to them controlling you, and you've given up.

Close your eyes and picture them dangling your life back and forth in front of your face. Then be brave and snatch it out of their hands. Once you have it in your hands hold onto it tight.

It's your life, and it belongs in your hands, not their hands. The day they hurt you they made you feel powerless but once you take your life back you'll feel powerful again. Always remember that you have to clean up the mess that others make in your life. Cleaning up the mess won't be easy, but you have to pick up the pieces one at a time until your life is clean. If your life is a mess, clean it up.

1. Did you snatch your life back?

2. Were you afraid to snatch it?

3. Do you have your life back in your hands or is it still in their hands?

Claim Victory

Realize that you're at war with something that you've already defeated. You defeated your past and left it behind. However, you never claimed victory. You won against the person that hurt you, but you haven't claimed victory yet. You might not think you've won, but you have. The winner is the person that's still standing at the end of the fight. The past is over and guess who's still standing? You! Sure you were wounded, and those wounds still hurt, but you're still standing. The past is gone, but you're still here. The person who hurt you is in the past, but you're still here. You're still here, and you're still moving forward. You think you can't move on, but the truth is every time you get out of bed you're fighting and you're slowly moving on. However, you haven't claimed victory yet. The reason you haven't claimed victory is because you still see yourself as a victim. Realize that you're a survivor, not a victim. You were a victim at one point, but once you decided to keep living you became a survivor. You have been through a lot in life but you still continue to move forward. However, you still see yourself as a victim and not a survivor.

Ladies and Gentleman. I would like to introduce you to a person that survived their past. A person that has been through hell, but they're still standing. A person that still finds a way to smile even though they have every right to be sad. A person that has felt like giving up, but they still get out of bed every morning. The person I'm introducing you to is YOU. Now, get up here and claim victory. You've won against your past and your enemies because you're still STANDING. Be proud of yourself, and from now on call yourself a survivor, and not a victim.

Getting through your past was hard, and it still hurts, but you've gotten through it. It was one of the most difficult parts of your life, but you're still alive and kicking. You've won a fight that you didn't think you'd win. Yet, you haven't claimed victory. Hold your head up high, and claim victory. You've won your past wars, and you'll continue to win any other wars that your enemies throw at you

You're in a boxing ring, and you're fighting against an enemy. Your enemy keeps punching and kicking you, but at the end of the fight, you're still standing. The referee comes over to you, grabs your arm, raises it in the air, and says champion.

Right now you're hurting because the punches and kicks were painful, but you should also be proud of yourself for winning the fight. From now on when you win against your enemies claim VICTORY instead of defeat.

Have you claimed victory or defeat?

Never forget that you're the one that's still standing.

"Don't let your past hold you back in life. You SURVIVED and DEFEATED your past. I know it still hurts, but you WON that fight.

PICK YOUR STORY

Which of the following stories will be your life story?

1. You had a bad past, but you survived it, and then you let your past and your enemies STOP you from living your life to the fullest. You gave up on happiness, you gave up on yourself, and you were miserable your entire life.

2. You had a bad past, but you survived it, but you didn't let your past or your enemies STOP you from living your life to the fullest. You found a way to be happy again, you reached your goals, and you enjoyed the rest of your life.

Which story did you pick?

Which story would you want to read?

You're the boss of your life, and your story is your choice. Don't I repeat don't let your enemies DECIDE this for you. Be strong and make this your decision.

"The greatest stories aren't about people with a perfect past, there about people who survived a bad past, lived their dream, and had a happy ending." I want this to be your story.

Life isn't fair

Life is far from fair. Sometimes you'll have to go through things a person should never have to go through. Sometimes you'll feel as if you can't go on, and that you'd rather just give up on everything. Sometimes you'll cry so much that you'll think you can't cry anymore. Sometimes you'll cry over the same thing over and over again. After you've been hurt your life changes, and usually it's for the worse. However, if you just give life another chance you'll realize that even though life isn't fair you can still enjoy it. Just because you've been through a few living nightmares it doesn't mean that you should give up on your dreams. Just because you have a dark past it doesn't mean that you can't have a bright future. Just because you had a horrible beginning it doesn't mean that you can't have a happy ending. Will you give yourself a chance at happiness or will you stay bitter for the rest of your life? It's your life, and what you do with your life is your choice.

Everything happens for a reason?

Is a phrase that I don't agree with. That phrase is used to explain away questions that people don't know the answer to. Telling someone that they've been victimized or hurt for a reason is like telling them that God wanted it to happen to them. It's like telling them that it was supposed to happen to them. Sometimes it does happen for reason, but most of the time it happens because of someone else's actions or bad choices. Sometimes you'll get hurt for no reason at all. Some people will hurt you for no reason, and leave you to deal with the pain. After you've been hurt the last thing you want to hear is that it was for a reason. How dare someone say that all the pain and suffering you're going through is for a reason? I won't be telling you anything like that in this guide because in order to move on a person must know the truth. Trying to make someone feel better with old sayings like 'it happened to you for a reason' doesn't work. When a person hears that saying they want to know the reason. So, they ask questions like "Why did it happen to me?" or "What was the reason?" 'It happened for a reason' leads to more questions and more questions lead to no closure. Most people hold onto the past because they need closure. That chapter in their life is still open. They're constantly analyzing that hurtful part of their life, and trying to rewrite it. However, they won't move on until they close that chapter in their life.

MOVING ON

Most people think that moving on means that you have to forget the past. People are always telling them to just forget about it or to just get over it. However, common sense will tell you that you can't erase your memories or just forget about them. If your brain is working properly you're going to remember your past especially the hurtful parts of it. So, I'm not going to tell you to forget about it because we both know that's impossible. If everyone could erase their memories, and just forget them moving on would be a piece of cake, but it isn't that simple. Secondly, most people think that once you move on it won't bother you anymore. However, you have to realize that a hurtful thing will always be a hurtful thing, but there are ways for you to get through it and move on. Ways that will make you happier even though you have every right to be sad. Moving on doesn't mean that it doesn't bother you anymore. It means that you've decided that you're not going to let what happened to you ruin your whole life. Moving on means that you've decided to take your life back, and you want to find a way to be happy.

However, you won't move on until you start from the beginning. The beginning is the part of your life that you're still stuck at. It's somewhere in the past, and you won't move on until you leave the beginning of the story, and move to the present.

STEP TWO

is to realize that it wasn't your fault. The worst thing you can do is blame yourself for what they did to you.

Do you believe that you could have stopped them from hurting you? Chances are you believe that you could have stopped this from happening to you, and you've rewritten your past over and over again in your head. The rewritten version of your past blames you for what happened to you. The rewritten version also gives you a list of ways that you could have stopped this from happening to you.

When some people get hurt they rewrite their past, and they make themselves the bad guy. Or they blame what happened to them on something they've said or done in the past. In the real story they were the helpless victim who was hurt by the bad guy, but in the rewritten version they're the victim that could have stopped this from happening to them. However, since they couldn't or didn't stop this from happening to them they think it's their fault. Starting today I need you to believe and accept the real story.

The real story is:

1. You didn't know they were going to hurt you so you couldn't have stopped them.
2. They were the bad guy, and you were the good guy.
3. Nothing you did or said made this happen to you.
4. You were their victim, and you couldn't stop them from hurting you.
5. They took advantage of you, used you or abused you.
6. You were a kid and someone took advantage of your innocence.

You might be upset at the above statements, but it's the truth. You couldn't stop this from happening to you because it wasn't your choice. If it was your choice, it wouldn't have happened to you. You're hurt because someone else made the decision to hurt you. The choice they made hurt you to the core, and you're mad at yourself for not being able to stop it from happening to you. Will you accept the real story or will you continue to rewrite the story? When you accept the real story you admit that you were a helpless victim who was hurt by a bad guy. When you accept the rewritten story; you were the victim who could have stopped the bad guy from hurting you. Until you accept the real story you won't move on. The real story hurts, but it's what really happened. The rewritten story puts the blame on the victim who didn't do or say something to stop it from happening to them. The real story puts the blame on the bad guy who hurt the victim without giving the victim a choice in the matter.

From now on when you think about your past don't say the following 2 statements:

1. If I had done this or that it wouldn't have happened to me.

2. It wouldn't have happened to me if I hadn't of said that or done this.

When you say the above statements you are blaming yourself for what happened to you. When you catch yourself saying the above statements stop yourself, and remind yourself that you didn't do anything wrong that day, that month or that year.

What you did in the past wasn't wrong, but what they did to you in the past was wrong. So, instead of saying the above statements say *"I didn't do anything wrong. I was hurt because someone else took advantage of me, hurt me, used me or abused me. What happened to me was their choice, not mine. Nothing I did or said caused it to happen to me. They were the bad guy, and I was the good guy.."*

Do you blame what they've done to you on something you've said or done in the past? If so, you've rewritten the story to make yourself the bad guy who caused this to happen to you. Starting today I need you to make them the bad guy in your story and blame them for what happened to you.

It's not fair to blame yourself for what they did to you:

- If a grown up hurt you when you were a kid it's not your fault. How can a kid defend themselves against a grown up? You were a kid, and no-one should hurt a kid. It's not your fault that a grown up took advantage of your innocence.
- If someone you loved and trusted hurt you. It's not your fault that they couldn't be trusted or that they were a bad person.
- If you were raped by someone you know or a stranger, it's not your fault that someone took advantage of you. Just because someone is drunk or wearing sexy clothes it doesn't mean that they deserve to be raped.
- If a stranger hurt you it's not your fault that you were minding your own business, and some stranger decided to hurt you.

It's not fair when other people blame the victim, and it's not fair when you blame victims like yourself either. So, don't do it! Always be fair to yourself! Show yourself the same sympathy and empathy that you show others.

People rewrite their past because:

1. They'd rather be the victim who defeated the bad guy instead of the victim who couldn't defeat the bad guy.
2. They'd rather be the hero in their story instead of the helpless victim
3. The real story makes them feel weak or vulnerable, but the rewritten story makes them feel powerful
4. The real story is harder to deal with than the rewritten story.
5. Thinking of ways that they could have protected themselves from the bad guy makes them feel like they're not a helpless victim.

Assignment 2: Change the story back to how it really happened:

Grab your pen and paper and rewrite what happened, placing the blame on them

I didn't do anything wrong that day THEY did something wrong. I'm innocent, and they're the bad guy.

Make them the bad guy in your story. Take the blame off of you, and put it on them. Everything you've blamed on yourself needs to be blamed on them. What happened to you was their fault, and they should be punished for it instead of you. Write your real story in your journal. In the real story I want you to make them the bad guy, and you the good guy. The real story must not blame you for anything that they did to you. As soon as you think that something you said or did caused it to happen to you remind yourself that what you did wasn't bad, but what they did was bad.

Don't blame yourself for the hateful, mean or sick actions of someone else. No matter what happened to you it wasn't your fault.

Who hurt you? They did! So, take the blame off of you, and put it on them. You can control your actions, but you can't control someone else's actions. So, if someone hurts you blame them because they made the decision to do it. You might think it's your fault because of something you've said or done, but it's not your fault. You might think it's your fault because they're blaming it on you, but it's not your fault. What happened to you wasn't your choice it was their choice. If you had a choice it would not have happened to you, but you didn't have a choice they just did it without your permission. Did you give them permission to hurt you? No! So, stop blaming yourself for what they did to you. From now on I want you to stop blaming yourself for what others do to you without your permission.

"If you didn't give them permission to hurt you there's no way that it could be your fault"

"Just because you were a victim that day, month or year it doesn't mean that you have to be a victim the rest of your life."

"Everyone will be hurt by someone. Expect to be hurt sometimes, but don't let what happens to you turn you into someone that you're not."

Whose fault is it that you were hurt? ______________________________

Complete the below sentences

1. I Blame them for

   ____

   ____

   ____

   ____

2. It wasn't my fault because

____

____

____

STEP THREE

is to blame them for what happened to you. What happened to you was their fault and their choice. They shouldn't have hurt you, and they deserve to be punished for what they did to you. They might have gotten away with it, but they still deserve to be punished because what they did to you was wrong. They were a horrible person, and they shouldn't have taken advantage of you, and messed up your past. It's their fault that you're in so much pain, and it's their fault that you're so miserable. What they did to you will not go unpunished. They will pay for what they did to you at some point in their life. What goes around comes around, and their turn will come up. Karma will take care of them just move on and take care of yourself. I know you want to see them suffer for what they've done to you, but getting revenge on them won't make your pain and suffering go away. You might think it will, but even if they were punished for what they've done to you it wouldn't undo what they've done to you. Also, even if they were punished for what they've done to you it wouldn't change the fact that they've left you to deal with it. That's right! You're the one that has to fix yourself and your life. They're not going to fix it, revenge isn't going to fix it, and no-one else is going to fix it. Even though they're the one that broke you, you have to be the one that puts yourself back together. It's not fair, but that's the only way to get your life back, and it's the only way to get through this. I know you want revenge, but you have to realize that getting revenge won't change what they've already done to you. Getting revenge won't change the past or take away the pain you feel inside. The best revenge you can get on them is to move on with your life. If you give up on yourself, your life or love because of them, they win. If you move on, chase after your goals and try to be happy, you win. Moving on shows them that they might have hurt you, but they didn't destroy you or ruin your chance of ever being happy.

Whose fault is it that you were hurt? ____________________________

Will getting revenge on them change anything? If so, what?

____

____

STEP FOUR

is to realize that everything that happens to you isn't about you.

A person that has been through a lot in life might feel unlucky. They might feel as if they're doomed to fail in life, and that something about them causes them to fall, victim, numerous times. However, they should realize that the world is getting crazier and that more and more people are becoming selfish. During your lifetime you will have run-ins with crazy, bad, selfish, and all kinds of people who will hurt you just to get what they want. Just because they're no good it doesn't mean that you're no good. Some of the nicest people fall victim to some of the evilest people in the world. As I mentioned earlier life isn't fair, and some things will happen to you that shouldn't happen to you. However, you just have to pick up the pieces and move on. After something bad happens to you, you have two choices. You can give up or you can keep fighting. If you're not fighting that means you've given up. Never define yourself by how others treat you. Just because a monster hurts you it doesn't mean that you're a bad person. It means that you're a person that was wronged. Never let what happens to you make you think that something is wrong with you.

When people get hurt they think that something about them made it happen to them. They think that something must be wrong with them for something like that to happen to them. Realize that everything that happens to you isn't about you. They hurt you because they're crazy, angry, bitter, evil, and mean or for some other reason. No matter why they hurt you, just know that it wasn't about you. You were just their target or their victim. You were just someone for them to use, take their anger out on or take advantage of. Nothing you did or said caused them to hurt you; they just did it because they wanted to. It happened to you because something is wrong with them or they were being selfish. It had nothing to do with you! They hurt you for their own selfish reasons. Again, their actions are their fault, not yours.

"Realize that some people only care about their needs, and they don't care who they have to hurt to get their needs met"

TWO SIDES OF YOU

There are two sides of you; the optimistic side of you yearns for inner peace and true happiness and the pessimistic side of you is stuck in your past where it has become comfortable. The pessimistic side of you lurks in the shadows and doesn't believe that you can ever be truly happy. However, the optimistic side of you is hoping that you will find a way to move on so that it can be truly happy. Every time the optimistic side of you is extremely happy, the pessimistic side rears it's doubtful head and tells you that it won't last and that something bad will happen to you again. The pessimistic side holds the optimistic side back in life; every time it has a great idea or wants to do something exciting, the pessimistic side shoots it down. The pessimistic side of you sounds like a bad person but it's far from bad. That side of you is really hurt and in pain. So, it does everything it can to stop you from being hurt again.

1. It doesn't want you to feel like a failure so it stops you from trying something new.
2. It doesn't want people to judge you so it tells you not to do anything that will cause you to get judged.
3. It doesn't want you to get hurt so it tells you not to trust anyone
4. It doesn't allow you to enjoy happy moments because it's preparing you for whatl might happen next.

It's just trying to protect you. However, you need to let it know that you don't need it to protect you anymore and that you don't blame it for what happened to you in the past. It's like an overprotective mom, watching out for you. In order to move on you have to spread your wings and fly without the fear of being hurt or failing or falling or being rejected. You can't live in fear. Letting the pessimistic side of you control your life holds you back in life. Start letting the optimistic side of you make the decisions. The optimistic side wants to explore, it wants to be free, it's tired of living in the past, it wants to reach its goals, it wants to be happy, it wants its chains removed and it wants the pessimistic side of you to know that it will be okay.

The optimistic side of you is the side that wants to move on, will you let it?

If so read the below message out loud. Reading out loud is important because hearing your own voice, helps it to remain in your memory.

Dear pessimistic side of me,

thanks for protecting me, but I want to be free now. I want to chase my goals and dreams and live my life without chains and constant fear. I want you to know that if I fall, I am capable of getting back up. I want you to know that if I fail, I am capable of trying it again and again until I succeed. I want you to know that if I get hurt again, that I'm capable of surviving it, just like I survived the things in my past. I know you're afraid but it's time to move on and find true happiness. I'm giving you my hand to hold because from now on I will be guiding us in the direction that I want us to go

Sincerely me, the optimistic side. I love you and again thanks for looking out for me.

STEP FIVE

is to realize that you have the right to cry. If you've been hurt, you should cry because that's what people do when they're in pain. Cry until you can't cry anymore. Crying doesn't mean that you're weak or that you're a crybaby, it means you're hurting inside, and you're releasing your pain through your tears. There's nothing wrong with crying, but after you're done I want you to find something in your life to smile about.

If you've been holding back your tears, it's time to release them. Allowing your body to soothe itself helps you to move on, and cope with what has happened to you.

If you keep crying over the same thing over and over again. That 1 thing is keeping you stuck in the past, and that 1 thing is one of the hardest things you've ever had to go through. Until you close the chapter in your life that keeps bringing those tears to your eyes you'll continue to live in the past.

1. Do you have the right to be angry?

2. Do you have the right to cry?

3. Do you have the right to be sad?

STEP SIX

is to realize that you have every right to be angry.

When you're mad at someone you want them to do one or more of the following things to satisfy your emotional needs:

1. Acknowledge your feelings
2. Admit that they're wrong
3. Apologize
4. Get punished for what they've done to you
5. Give you a reason for why they did it

And you stay mad at them until they've satisfied your emotional needs.

However, you have to realize that a stranger or someone that doesn't care about you won't do any of the above things. So, you have to find a way to let go of your anger without their help. They're not going to apologize. They're not going to admit that they're wrong. They're not going to acknowledge your feelings or empathize with you, and they might not be punished for what they've done to you. Also, since there's no excuse for bad behavior the only reason they'll give you is an excuse that they've made up. When someone loves you they satisfy your emotional needs when you're mad at them because they love you, and they want your forgiveness. However, the person that hurt you doesn't love you. So, you have to satisfy your own emotional needs, and get rid of your anger without their help.

You have every right to be angry or upset with them. They shouldn't have hurt you, and what they did to you was wrong. However, you have to realize that the anger you feel towards them is keeping you in the past. You're holding onto the anger because that's your only way of punishing them for what they did to you. However, holding onto the anger isn't punishing them it's punishing you. Your anger is making you bitter, miserable and angry, but your anger isn't doing anything to them at all. That's right! The person you want to punish isn't being punished by your anger.

You've been holding all of that anger in because you want to take it out on them and punish them for what they've done to you. But you've only punished yourself. The person you're mad at is in your past, but you're still letting them control your present life. They still have power over you, and they'll continue to have power over you until you let go of all of that built up anger you have towards them.

Once you let go of your anger towards them they'll no longer have power over you or your emotions. To let go of the anger you have to decide whether you're going to control your emotions or whether you're going to let them control your emotions. Every time you catch yourself getting upset at what they've done to you realize that you are letting them control your emotions and try to get back in control of it.

The main reason people don't let go of anger is because they want the person who hurt them to pay for what they've done to them. Realize that letting go of your anger doesn't mean that they've won or that they've gotten away with hurting you, it means that you've decided that you're not going to let what they've done to you control you anymore.

Before you go to step 7 do the following assignment

Assignment 3: Read the letter below out loud.

Dear Person Who Hurt Me:

I'm mad at you for hurting me, and I'd love to get revenge on you for what you've done to me. But I've decided that I will no longer waste any more of my time on you. Starting right now, I'm going to use my time to move on with my life so that I can be happy. You ruined my past, but I will not let you ruin my future. You ruined my past, but you can't ruin my future because I won't let you do it. You've already caused enough damage in my life and I refuse to let you cause any more damage. You've made me miserable in the past, but I'm going to do whatever it takes so that I can be happy right now and in my future. I'm moving on with my life, and I'm leaving you in the past where you belong. Starting right now I will slowly release the anger I have towards you. Not because I'm over what you've done to me or because I agree with what you've done to me, but because I'm done letting what you've done to me control my life. I'm releasing this anger because I am no longer going to let you control my life and my emotions anymore. I've been through a lot in my life, but I'm still alive and I'm still standing because I am a strong person. What you did to me hurt me, but I won't let it destroy me because I'm too strong to let that happen. I've gotten through other things in life and I'll get through this too because I am strong. Don't think you've gotten away with it though because Karma will pay you a visit one day, and when she does you'll get what you deserve.

Signed by Me. The person that's moving on with their life.

"Let go of your anger because it's hurting you instead of the person you want to take your anger out on."

STEP SEVEN

is to stop letting them control you. To move on you have to decide whether you're going to let them control your life or whether you're going to control it yourself. Do you want the person who hurt you to control your life? Of course not, but if you've given up on love because of what they've done to you you're letting them control you.

1. If you're angry and bitter because of what they've done to you, you're letting them control your emotions.
2. If you're taking your anger out on other people because of what they've done to you, you're letting them control you.
3. If you're afraid to trust anyone because of what they've done to you, you're letting them control you
4. If you've given up on your goals, life or dreams because of them you're letting them control your life and mess up your future.

The person who hurt you shouldn't be controlling your life. Are you going to let them control your life forever? They've already messed up your past, and now you're letting what they've done to you mess up your present life and your future. It's going to be hard, but you need to get back in control of your life. Your life and future should be in your hands not their hands.

Before you go to step nine do the following assignment

Assignment 4: Picture the person that hurt you in your head and read the following letter out loud.

Dear: Person who hurt me in the past

Starting today I'm taking my life back from you. What you did to me hurt me, but I will not let it destroy me. I will not let what you've done to me ruin my whole life. Starting right now I'm going to control my own life. Starting right now I will live my life by my rules. Starting right now I will not let what you've done to me ruin my chance at finding love. I will not let what you've done to me stop me from being happy. I will not let what you've done to me stop me from chasing my goals and dreams. I will not give up on myself because of you. I will not be bitter and angry because of you. Starting right now I am in control of my life.

Signed by me. The boss of my life.

*Name*________________________________ *Date* ________________

Who's going to control your life from now on? Them or you? ________________

Step eight

is to realize that the past is over. You can't change it, you can't erase it, and nothing you do or say will make it go away. If you could change your past you would do it in a heartbeat, but you can't. If you could erase that part of your life you'd be so much happier right now, but you can't erase it. You can't erase your past or change it, but you can survive your past and that's something that you've already done. You didn't erase your past or change it, but you did survive it, and that says a lot about you.

Some people waste too much time thinking of ways that they could have changed something in their past. When they should be using their time to change something in their present life. The past can't be changed, but the present can and that's what you should be focusing on.

Below are 3 things people say when they're thinking of ways that they could have changed their past.

1. If I had said this it wouldn't have happened to me.
2. If I had done this they wouldn't have hurt me.
3. I could have stopped this from happening to me if I had said or done this.

If you catch yourself thinking of ways you could have stopped this from happening to you remind yourself that it's over, and you have already gotten through it. Even though it was one of the hardest things you have ever had to go through, you have already made it through it. You can't change the past, but you were strong enough to make it through it, and that's something you should be proud of. Even though you were thrown a curve ball you still knocked the ball out of the park.

1. If you spend your entire day thinking about what you should have done in the past, what will you accomplish?
2. If you spend your entire day thinking about what you can do NOW to better your life, what will you accomplish?
3. Which of the above will you do? It's up to you. It's your life.

"You don't have the power to erase your past, and you don't have the power to change your past. However, you do have the power to survive your past, and the power to move on"

You can't change the past. So, there's no point in thinking about what you should have said or done differently.

"Focusing on what you could have said or done in the past is a waste of time. Use your time to fix the things you can change right now."

"You can't change the past, but if you change the present you'll have a better future."

"They ruined your past, but they can't ruin your future unless you let them"

"Don't focus on what you should have done before focus on what you should be doing now."

THE WHY ME'S

Some people hold onto the past because they want closure for what happened to them.

1. They want to know why someone hurt them.
2. They want to know why something happened to them.

3. They want to know why someone betrayed them, used them, neglected them, abused them or raped them etc.

4. If they're religious they want to know why God didn't stop it from happening to them.

If someone you loved left you they might not have meant to hurt you, but they just weren't in love with you. They can't make themselves love you. It hurts, but you have to realize that they're the wrong person for you. If they were right for you, they wouldn't have left you. Don't think something is wrong with you just realize that they were wrong for you.

If someone cheated on you, abused you, raped you, molested you, betrayed you, used you or took advantage of you. Realize that they hurt you for their own selfish reasons. You didn't cause it to happen to you. They just took advantage of you, violated you, or disrespected you for their own selfish reason.

Realize that the only answer the person who hurt you can give you is an excuse. If you ask them why they hurt you they'll make up an excuse or they'll blame it on you. There's no excuse for bad behavior. They're grown and they know right from wrong they just chose to treat you wrong.

Right now I'm fixing to give you the only answer you need for WHY they did it to you.

They did it because they wanted to. They did it for their own selfish reasons. They knew it was wrong but they did it anyway.

Will you accept the truth or will you continue to ask WHY because you're hoping that someone will give you a good excuse for WHY it happened to you. If I were you I'd want the truth because there's no excuse for bad behavior.

A good excuse will make you feel better, but the truth will make you realize that they were just a bad person, and they hurt you for no reason. All that pain you're going through was caused by someone who only cared about what they wanted. It's okay to want answers or search for answers, but sometimes you have to realize that you HAVE all the answers you need. You might not like the answers, but you have them.

Don't blame God for what they did because God didn't tell them to hurt you. Never blame God for someone else's sin. Nowhere in the bible did God say that it was okay to do half the things I mentioned above. So, if someone does those things they're going against Gods plan for you.

For example; Thou shall not commit murder is one of the Ten Commandments. When someone goes to a school and kills kids they are breaking Gods commandment and going against Gods plan for those kids. If that person hadn't broken Gods commandment those kids would still be alive.

In your everyday life, you might be used to people hurting you, apologizing for it, and telling you why they did it. However, you have to realize that sometimes people will hurt you without giving you an apology or a reason, but you still have to find a way to move on.

"It's not fair to blame God for someone else's sin."

"Bad things will happen to you, but you can't let it ruin your whole life"

You think you can't move on without knowing WHY they hurt you but you can. Again if you ask them WHY they hurt you all they'll tell you is a list of LIES and EXCUSES. Do you need to hear a list of their lies and excuses? No, you don't. You don't need to hear it. What's the point in listening to a list of their lies and excuses? They did it for an inexcusable, selfish reason. No matter what they'd say to you it won't be a good reason because there's NO excuse for bad behavior. If they told you a list of lies and excuses for WHY they hurt you what would that change? Nothing at all. The only thing it will do is make you feel worse because you'll realize that you were hurt for no reason at all and that the person that hurt you is making excuses for what they did to you. So, all you need to know is that they were wrong, that it wasn't your fault, that you didn't deserve and that you're still here. Nothing they've done or said to you has stopped you yet. You were strong enough to survive what they did.

Don't ask them WHY they hurt you because all they'll tell you is LIES and EXCUSES. There's no excuse for what they've done. You don't need to hear any of their lies and excuses. Just know that they were WRONG, and try to move on. You know that they were wrong, and that's all that matters.

3. Do you need to know why they hurt you? _______________

4. Realize that you don't need an apology, you are strong enough to move on without an apology or an explanation. There's no excuse for what they've done to you.

5. Do you need an apology or an explanation from them? __________________

6. Is what happened to you, your fault? _______________

7. Is what happened to you God's fault _________________

STEP NINE

is to stop being the victim. Realize that you have every right to feel sorry for yourself. What happened to you shouldn't have happened to you, and you have every right to be sad. However, you also have to realize that feeling sorry for yourself keeps you stuck in the past, and it doesn't change anything.

If you stay in victim mode, feeling sorry for yourself, and feeling miserable will become comfortable to you. Once it becomes comfortable to you you'll become addicted to feeling pain. When someone is addicted to feeling pain, they constantly focus on the bad things that have happened to them so they can feel sorry for themselves. When someone is addicted to feeling pain or feeling hurt they intentionally drift off into the past just so they can feel the pain they felt before all over again. When they feel the pain they become the victim all over again, and they enter into victim mode. Victim mode is different from flashbacks. Flashbacks or old memories pop up randomly, but victim mode is entered into willingly and purposefully. The pain addict purposefully focuses on bad memories just to relive those old feelings. It's kind of like a drug addict that needs their fix so they can get high. Only the person that's addicted to feeling pain does it to feel low and miserable. They're addicted to feeling hurt, and feeling pain so they dredge up old memories to get their fix.

To get over this addiction you need to stop seeing yourself as a victim. When you see yourself as a victim you believe that you can't control anything in your life, but that is far from the truth. You can control a lot of things in your life. Just because you couldn't stop that person from hurting you it doesn't mean that you can't control other things in your life.

Starting today I need you to be your own hero and save yourself from all the misery you're drowning in. Starting right now I want you to stop calling yourself a victim, and I want you to start calling yourself a survivor. You have survived your past, and you're trying your best to fight and move on. So, you're a survivor, not a victim. Just because you were a victim once it doesn't mean that you have to be a victim all of your life. When you catch yourself feeling sorry for yourself focus on something that makes you happy.

If you believe that you are addicted to being in victim mode, you have to stop yourself from entering into it. Usually, people drift off into victim mode when they are already sad about something, when they're lonely or when they feel like they've been victimized again. They do this because what's happening to them in the present reminds them of being, unloved, unwanted or hurt just like they were in the past.

Example;

Max's boss gave someone else the promotion that he wanted. Max felt that he deserved the promotion and that his boss was being unfair to him. When Max got home he sat on the couch, and begin to think of all the times that people were unfair to him. He closed his eyes, and drifted off into his childhood, his teen years, and college years. He thought about all his current problems, and anything else that he could think of that seemed unfair. Dredging up all of those past memories gave Max instant pain, and the pain made him feel like a victim once again.

In the above example, Max didn't have a flashback of his past, he purposefully dredged up his past just to feel like a victim again. Also, Max went from being sad about not getting a promotion to being sad about everything that has ever happened to him. Don't be a Max. When something bad happens to you or you feel hurt deal with it without dredging up the past. Piling all of your life problems into one pile will cause you to be depressed. If someone hurts you don't dredge up every memory of yourself being hurt by someone. Try your best to stay in the present.

Do you constantly remind yourself of your past? When something bad happens to you do you drift off into the past, and think of all of the bad things that have ever happened to you? Do you pile your past and present problems into one pile? If your memories pop up randomly you're not a pain addict. If you're constantly reminding yourself of it chances are you're a pain addict.

Read and follow the steps below to get rid of this addiction:

1. Admit that you intentionally drift off into the past when you're sad or lonely or feel unloved or when you feel unwanted.

2. Admit that you constantly focus on the bad things in your life or past and that you intentionally make yourself relive past memories.

3. When you catch yourself drifting off into the past stop yourself as soon as possible and focus on something else.

4. Deal with what's bothering you instead of feeling sorry for yourself.

After you admit that you have this problem you'll slowly do it less and less because it's not as enjoyable once you know that you're doing it to yourself intentionally. Simply because you want to feel like a victim, and you know that a victim isn't supposed to be intentionally causing themselves to feel pain.

Signs you're in victim mode

1. You focused on your past or problems intentionally.

2. You feel sorry for yourself

3. You feel like a victim

4. You feel like life is unfair

5. You feel like your heart is breaking

6. You feel pain inside

7. You feel warm inside because of the pain

8. You feel depressed

9. You feel like you did when you were hurt

10. You can snap out of it just by focusing on something else

If you catch yourself drifting off into the past, focus on something that will make you happy or reach out and talk to someone. Wallowing in self-pity and misery will keep you stuck in the past. Starting right now I want you to be your hero instead of their victim. Every time you catch yourself drifting off into victim mode I want you to save yourself from that misery.

Everyone isn't addicted to feeling pain. Some people just have flashbacks or old memories that pop up every now and then that make them feel miserable.

No matter what sends you down memory lane try to stop yourself from going down it by focusing on something in your present life.

"Intentionally making yourself relive the past is torturing yourself"

"You're a survivor, not a victim, and if you survived your past you can survive anything else that happens to you."

"There's nothing wrong with feeling sorry for yourself, but you also have to do something about it or it will ruin your future."

Are you a victim or a survivor? ______________________________

STEP TEN

is to realize how strong you are. It takes a strong person to go through hell and make it out alive. It takes a strong person to move on after someone has hurt them to the core. It takes a strong person to move on after someone has broken their heart into a million pieces. It takes a strong person to keep going even though they feel like giving up. Some people don't realize how strong they are. If you've been through a lot and you're still standing you're stronger than you think you are. Feeling sad or crying about what happened to you doesn't mean that you're weak it's just your way of dealing with emotional pain. You're strong because you kept going after they hurt you. You're strong because you keep going even though it's hard to get up sometimes. You're strong because you keep going even though you cry yourself to sleep sometimes. You're strong because you keep going even though you feel weak sometimes. It takes a strong person to keep going despite it all. You might cry sometimes and you might feel sad sometimes, but you're a strong person. Never forget that.

You might feel as if you're weak, but that is far from the truth. If you were weak you wouldn't have survived your past. You're a greater, stronger, braver person than you think you are. Nothing and no-one has stopped you from living another day. Yet you still see yourself as weak and as a victim??

Activity: Put down your device and raise both of your arms in the air, and say the following out loud "I WON THE FIGHT AGAINST MY PAST AND MY ENEMIES. I WON"

Don't go to step eleven until you've completed the above activity. From now on I want you to think of yourself as a great, strong, brave person instead of a weak person. You're far from weak. Give yourself credit where it's due.

"Strong people cry sometimes, fall sometimes and feel like giving up sometimes, but what makes them strong is that they keep on going anyway."

"A strong person keeps moving forward despite what happens to them"

Are you a strong person? _____________

STEP ELEVEN

is to decide whether you're going to be bitter or whether you're going to be happy. You can't choose both. If you stay bitter you're letting them control you and your life. If you move on you become the boss of your life again and you can chase after happiness. Don't let what they did to you take away your right to be happy. You're a good person, and you have the right to be happy. If you want to be happy you have to let go of the bitterness. Let go of your bitterness for you, not for them. This isn't about them; it's about you getting your life back.

Some people think they can't be happy anymore because they think what happened to them is too hard to get over, but they can. They can be happy they just have to get back in control of their life. The person who hurt you is controlling your life and ruining your chance at happiness. And you're letting them do it.

Fight for your right to be happy. If you give up, they win. If you fight or move on you win. Don't let them win! They made your past a living hell, but you can make your future a happy place if you take your life back. Are you going to take your life back or are you going to let them win? Don't let what they did to you change you into a bitter, angry person. Stay true to yourself and who you really are.

Activity: Grab your journal for this activity. **Important Activity don't skip.**

Life is one of the toughest Professors you'll ever have, and it will constantly test your strength. Let's see if you passed Life's test.

Write down 5 hurtful things that you've been through.

1. ____

2. ____

3. ____

4. ____

5. ____

At the end of Step 12 finish this activity.

"Your past might be miserable, but your future can be full of happiness if you don't give up."

"Don't let the bad things that happened to you make you miss out on the good things that could happen to you"

"Your past might be messed up, but you can't stay broken forever. Find a way to fix yourself."

Are you going to fight for happiness or are you going to give up and be miserable? It's your life and it's up to you?

STEP TWELVE

is to realize that your past doesn't have to define who you are. Just because something bad happened to you it doesn't mean that you're a bad person. It just means that you're a good person that has been wronged. From now focus on who you are as a person instead of what they did to you. What are some good things about you?

- Maybe you're a good person who's always there for their friends.
- Maybe you're a good mom or dad.
- Maybe you're smart, funny or witty
- Maybe you have an awesome talent or awesome career
- Maybe you're good at fixing things or creating things

Focus on all the good things about you instead of the bad things that have happened to you. No matter what happens to you never let anyone take away the good things about you. People will hurt you, but they can't take away the good things about you unless you let them.

Some people constantly focus on the bad things about themselves and their life, and then they wonder why they're so miserable. I guess you've forgotten that there are some good things about you too. A bad thing happened to you, but it doesn't change the fact that you're a good person. Give yourself a break from all that misery. Use all of your strength and break free from it so you can be happy.

Don't let what happened to you change your personality. If you're a nice person stay nice. If you become bitter you're letting them control your life and you're letting them ruin your chance of finding happiness.

"People will hurt you, but don't let it make you bitter, and don't give up on finding someone better"

"Bad things will happen to you, but don't let it ruin your whole life"

BELOW WRITE DOWN 5 GOOD THINGS ABOUT YOU

1.

2.

3.

4.

5.

ACTIVITY: Life's test continued.

1. Grab your journal or go back to step 11 and look at the five hurtful things that you've been through
2. Put a check mark next to everything that you've SURVIVED.
3. If you're reading this you're still alive and you've survived everything on your list.
4. So, put a check mark next to everything on your list. Your score 100%

Basically, you've passed all the test that Professor Life has thrown at you. Some of the tests were heartbreaking, painful, and hurtful, you name it, but you still passed them. Look at your list and be proud of how strong you are. Stop letting that list control your life. If you passed all of those tests, then you can pass any other test that Professor Life throws at you. Once you survive anything, add it to your list of things that you've already DEFEATED.

Did you survive everything that has happened to you? ___________________________

Are you a survivor or a victim? ____________________________________

STEP THIRTEEN

is to stop using what happened to you as an excuse to avoid moving on with your life. What happened to you is life changing, but it doesn't have to be life ruining. What happened to you doesn't have to ruin your whole life. What happened to you can't ruin your whole life unless you let it. I know bad things have happened to you, but you can't let a few bad things ruin everything else in your life. If you keep fighting good things will happen to you too. If you chase your goals your dreams will come true. If you give love another chance you will fall in love again.

Starting today I want you to stop using what happened to you as an excuse for giving up on yourself and your life. What happened to you is a good excuse to hate life, but it's not a good excuse to give up on someone you're supposed to love. So, if you love yourself never give up on yourself. When you love someone you don't turn your back on them when they need you the most and right now is when you need yourself the most. Love yourself by helping yourself to get through this. Give yourself a chance to be happy.

"Don't let what they did to you that day, hour or year ruin your whole life. Find a way to move on so you can be happy"

"Never give up on yourself! You should never give up on someone you're supposed to love."

Are you going to give up on your goals and dreams because of what happened to you or are you going to fight for your goals and dreams? It's your life and it's up to you.

STEP FOURTEEN

is to start caring about yourself and your life again. Some people give up on themselves after something bad happens to them. They stop taking care of their health, their body, and their responsibilities. They stop chasing their goals and dreams. They give up on everything that could make them happy, and they settle for everything that makes them miserable. In relationships, they put up with people who don't care about them, and in life, they put up with things that make them miserable.

When you don't care about yourself you give up on life emotionally. Physically you're alive, but mentally you've already given up on yourself and ended your life.

Starting right now I want you to start caring about yourself again. Don't give up on yourself because of what they did to you. I know what they did to you hurts, but giving up on yourself isn't punishing them it's punishing you. When you don't care about yourself you punish yourself by letting people hurt you over and over again, and by giving up on everything that could make you happy.

Below are 5 ways that people punish themselves:

1. When you give up on your goals you're punishing yourself because you're forcing yourself to live a life that you don't want to live.

2. When you give up on love, you're punishing yourself because you're giving up your chance of finding love.
3. When you stop taking care of yourself you're punishing yourself by messing up your health.
4. When you stay with someone that disrespects you you're punishing yourself by letting them hurt you over and over again.
5. When you give up on happiness, you're punishing yourself by making sure that you stay miserable forever.

Punishing yourself is your way of keeping yourself in victim mode. Victim mode is where you can feel sorry for yourself and feel miserable.

People who punish themselves are constantly doing things that will lead to them being miserable:

1. They stop taking care of themselves emotionally, mentally or physically which leads to them being miserable.
2. They stop chasing after things that will make them happy and they put up with things that make them miserable.
3. They stay with people that hurt them, use them, or abuse them which leads to them being miserable.
4. They stop chasing after their goals and settle for a life they don't want which leads to them being miserable.

A person who punishes themselves doesn't do it intentionally, they do it subconsciously. They do it because they want to create situations where they can feel sorry for themselves and stay in victim mode.

Assignment 5: Answer the following questions

1. Have you stopped taking care of yourself?

2. Are you putting up with people or things that make you miserable?

3. Have you given up on things that could make you happy?

4. Have you given up on your goals or dreams?

5. Are you a happy person or a miserable person?

6. Do you have a happy life or a miserable life?

7. Do you think you'll ever be happy?

8. Name something that you do that leads to you being miserable?

9. Name something that you don't do that leads to you being miserable?

10. Will you try to change your life so you can be happy?

11. Will you start taking care of yourself emotionally, mentally and physically?

12. Will you chase your goals and dreams so you can be happy?

13. Will you stop putting up with people that use you, abuse you and hurt you?

14. Will you stop putting up with things that make you miserable?

15. Will you give yourself a chance at happiness?

16. Will you fight for your life or will you give up?

You have the power to change almost everything in your life, but you also have the power not to change anything.
Which power will you use?

Stop punishing yourself because you don't deserve to be treated like that. Starting today I want you to stop punishing yourself for what they did to you, and I want you to start rewarding yourself for being a survivor. You've been miserable long enough and now it's time for you to be happy.

"Someone deserves to be punished, but that person isn't you. So, why are you punishing yourself?"

"Punishing yourself is like locking up an innocent person for what a guilty person has done. It's unfair!" Be fair to yourself.

Below are 5 ways that you can reward yourself

1. Reward yourself by chasing after your goals and dreams.
2. Reward yourself by giving love another chance.
3. Reward yourself by doing things that will make you happy instead of miserable.

4. Reward yourself by surrounding yourself with people who love you instead of people who hurt you.
5. Reward yourself by taking care of yourself physically, emotionally and mentally.
6. Reward yourself because you deserve to be happy for once.

Don't ever think about killing yourself. You were put on earth for a reason. There are so many things you can do with your life. You might feel empty, and you think no-one cares about you, but that's not true. A lot of good things can be waiting for you in the future. You might find love, you might have kids, and you might accomplish one of your goals. There are a lot of things you can do with your life. Maybe you can help other people who are going through what you're going through? Find a positive way to use your life. Don't give up just take things a day at a time.

Are you going to punish yourself for what they've done to you or are you going to reward yourself for being so brave and because you deserve to be happy? It's your life and it's up to you?

STEP FIFTEEN

is to let out your emotions. When you let them out it lifts a weight off of your shoulder and it keeps you from taking your anger out on other people. Some people hold in their emotions until they can't take any more pain, and then they take it out on someone they love or an innocent person. Release your anger in a positive way, not a negative way. It's not fair for you to hurt other people just because you're hurting inside. Next time you catch yourself about to explode on someone remind yourself that they don't deserve to be treated like that, and excuse yourself from the room.

Below are some healthy ways to release your anger

· Write your thoughts in a journal

· Join a support group

· Join an online forum and talk to people with similar issues

· Talk to your friends and family

· Talk to a therapist

· Go for a walk

· Exercise

· Take a vacation or a break

· Make a vlog

One of the things that helped me was, sharing my story. Don't be afraid to speak up and speak out. You have nothing to be ashamed of. The person that should feel ashamed is the person that hurt you. What happened to you doesn't have to be a burden or a secret that you have to hide and carry alone. Share your story with others that are in your shoes and you'll feel so much better and you won't feel alone.

Also, don't use alcohol or drugs to solve your problems or to avoid dealing with what happened to you. Doing that will make things worse and doing that won't solve the problem. The problem will still be there when you sober up and it won't go away until you face it, and deal with it. If you're addicted to drugs or alcohol get help. Don't throw your life away because of what they did to you. You're strong enough to get over your addiction. It will be one of the hardest things you'll ever have to do, but you're strong enough to do it. You owe yourself a chance at being happy.

Do you use drugs or alcohol to solve your problems?

If so, when will you research ways or programs that will help you with your addiction?

STEP SIXTEEN

is to be proud of yourself. If you're reading this guide that shows that you are taking steps to better your life. Be proud of yourself for making the decision to get your life back. Be proud of yourself for making it through your past and for trying to find ways to better your present life and your future. Considering what you've been through, you are on the right track and you're doing the best that you can.

Before going to step seventeen do the following assignment.

Assignment 6: Pat yourself on the back for making it through your past, and for trying your best to move on. You've been through a lot and you should be proud of yourself for making it through it.

Did you pat yourself on the back? _________________

I'm watching you. Pat yourself on the back. Show yourself some well-deserved love.

STEP SEVENTEEN

is to keep busy. Keep yourself busy by chasing after your goals and other things that will make you happy. If you keep yourself really busy you'll be so focused on the present that you'll barely have time to think about your past. When you're busy chasing after happiness you don't have time to mope around and be miserable. Keep busy and focus on things that are important to you.

1. Are you focusing on the past or the present?

2. Will you start focusing on the present?

3. What can you do today that will better your life?

4. What can you do tomorrow that will better your life?

5. What will make you happy?

6. Will you do these things? Yes, or no?

7. Do you deserve to be happy?

STEP EIGHTEEN

is to go out and create new memories. Go out and enjoy life. Do things you've never done before, and go places you've never been before. When you're out creating new memories you'll barely have time to think about your old memories. Sure the old memories will pop up every now and then, but the new memories you're creating will outweigh them. Think about the times you were out having fun with friends or family. During those happy times did you think about your miserable past? Nope, because you were too busy enjoying the present. If a person is extremely happy in the present, their miserable past will be left behind where it belongs.

1. What's something that you've always wanted to do?

2. What's your favorite memory?

3. What place would you like to vacation to?

4. Will you create new and fun memories?

5. Smile

6. I said smile

7. Did you smile?

8. Thanks

9. Have you had fun days where you laughed and enjoyed yourself?

Life isn't bad, it's the people in the world that make it bad sometimes, never forget that. You had fun in the past and you can still have fun and enjoy life in the present/future. Okay?

STEP NINETEEN

is to fight. You have to fight for your right to live and be happy. You only get one life and it's up to you whether it will be a great life or a miserable one. I know they messed up your past, but if you fight through this they can't mess up your future. This is your life, and I want you to fight for it. Give it everything you've got, and fight until you win your life back. Whether you know it or not you've already been fighting through this just by getting up every day. But now I want you to fight harder than you've ever fought before. Don't stop fighting until you're happy with your life.

- · Fight to accomplish your goals
- · Fight to win your life back
- · Fight for your right to be happy
- · Fight because you're a fighter and that's what fighters do

Turn your anger into strength and use it to fight and fight and fight.

"You're at war with your past, and to win this war you must fight. Give it all of your strength, and fight until you win."

"Will your enemies win this war or will you win it?"

1. Are you fighting for your goals and dreams?

2. Are you doing everything you can to make your life better?

3. If not, get busy, no excuses. Below write 5 things you're going to fight for, starting today.

4. I'm going to fight for

5. I'm going to fight for

6. I'm going to fight for

7. I'm going to fight for

8. I'm going to fight for

9. When will you start?

STEP TWENTY

is to realize that you're not alone. You're not alone thousands of people have been in your shoes, and some people are in your shoes right now. That's right! Somewhere in this world, someone has been in your shoes. Sometimes you might feel like you're alone, and that no-one knows your pain, but that's not true. If you search the web you'll find people who have been through what you've been through. Reach out and talk to them, and you won't feel like you're alone anymore.

Are you alone or are there others that have been in your shoes? ______________________

STEP TWENTY-ONE

is to not be afraid to trust people. I know you've been hurt before, but if you don't learn how to trust anyone you'll end up alone. You can learn how to trust again or you can die alone, it's your choice. Everyone in this world isn't out to get you. There are people out there who are nice just like you and they're looking for someone to love and care for. Don't be afraid to trust people, just keep your eyes open and cut them off if they lose your trust.

"Not trusting anyone can protect your heart from breaking again, but it will also stop you from finding love again"

Are you afraid to trust people? _______________

If so, that's understandable, but from now on I want you to give people a fair chance to earn your trust, everyone isn't out to hurt you. Will, you lower your walls just a little bit?

If you're single you have to realize that you have to trust someone one day or you won't find love. If you're in a relationship, you still need to work on your trust issues with others because it can still interfere with certain parts of your relationship.

STEP TWENTY-TWO

is to realize that you're going to get through this. It's going to take time and a lot of heartache and tears, but you'll get through this.

I know you're going to get through this because you are a strong person who has been through hell and made it out alive.

I know you're going to get through this because plenty of people have tried to bring you down, and yet you're still standing.

I know you're going to get through this because even though you feel like giving up sometimes you still keep going.

I know you're going to get through this because even though you cry yourself to sleep sometimes; you still get out of bed every morning.

You're going to get through this because you're not going to let the person who hurt you control your life anymore. You're going to get through this because starting today you are taking your life back, and you're going to move on to bigger and better things. You're a fighter not a quitter and that's why you're going to get through this.

Moving on will be one of the hardest things you'll ever have to do, but based on your history and your strength I know you can do it. Good luck on your journey. I wish you success and happiness.

"Life isn't fair. Sometimes you'll go through things a person should never have to go through, but you're strong enough to make it through it"

What happened to you was hurtful, and it was one of the most painful things you have ever been through, but you survived it, and you lived to tell about. Now, that's the definition of being STRONG.

If you're moving on, mark this day on your calendar and get started on your new journey. Good luck to you. Leave feedback and share with those you love.

The paperback version of this book can be written in, great for workshops, seminars, and lectures

If you like this guide, you'll love

25 Steps to Letting Go of Someone you love- For those who need help letting go of someone they love; an ex or someone they were dating.

35 Steps to Loving Yourself - If you don't love yourself you'll settle for less in love and in life. Get this guide and start loving yourself today.

29 STEPS to Getting Back on Your Feet - For those who need help getting back on the right track. This guide will change your life.

12 Steps To Learning How To Handle Rejection - Learn how to handle rejection in life and in love.

Letting Go Of Mr. Wrong. - A must have for women who are dating or in a bad relationship.

34 Steps To Losing Weight And Keeping It Off

How Women Can Avoid Getting Played

How Men Can Avoid Getting Played-

Dating Guide For Single Women

Dating Guide For Single Men

Made in the USA
Monee, IL
20 April 2022

95080804R00025